Coca Cola® Ham, Coca Cola® Cake & Other Coca Cola® Recipes

By Diana Loera

Copyrighted 2014

All rights reserved. All content in this book is copyrighted and may not be shared or distributed without the written consent of Diana Loera and Loera Publishing LLC.

Additional Books by Diana Loera

I am always looking for cool recipes and interesting topics. Below are some of my books. More are being researched and written every month.

Thank you for your interest in my books!

Summertime Sangria

Best Copycat Recipes on the Planet

Party Time Chicken Wing Recipes

Awesome Thanksgiving Leftovers Revive Guide

Best Venison Recipes

Meet Me at the County Fair – Fair Food Recipes

What is the Paleo Diet & Paleo Diet Recipe Sampler

12 Extra Special Summer Dessert Fondue Recipes

14 Extra Special Winter Holidays Fondue Recipes

USA Based Wholesale Directory 2014

Fast Start Guide to Flea Market Selling

I601A – Our Journey to Ciudad Juarez

Stop Hot Flashes Now

Please visit www.LoeraPublishing.com to view all titles and descriptions. Thank you.

Introduction

This book has been about thirty years in the making.

Since my teenage years, I've always been a Coca Cola drinker. I know there are others who like other brands but Coca Cola has always been my choice.

Many years ago at a family picnic, I tried a dessert recipe that included Coca Cola as an ingredient and from that point, I was hooked on finding and testing dessert recipes with Coca Cola as an ingredient.

When I was older and married, my sister in law gave me a chicken recipe (included in this book) and that really sparked my interest as now I had a recipe for poultry whereas before all I had come across was dessert recipes.

So I kept looking and gathering recipes over the years. It has definitely been a fun project as I look back on all the recipes.

All the recipes in this book, with the exception of one uses Coca Cola.

The one that doesn't uses Diet Coke – it is a brownie recipe.

You'll see that there are in some cases variations of recipes for roast, ham, chicken, cake and others.

There are two meatloaf recipes, a Hungarian goulash and other unique recipes.

I suggest using Coca Cola at room temperature unless otherwise indicated.

I also suggest, always checking with guests for food allergies before serving or planning a menu. My granddaughter has nut allergies and it has really made me aware of always checking ingredients with others before giving them food.

Please note that the softcover edition of this book is 8 ½ x 11 in size. I also included some color photographs. The more photos I add, the more that it drives the printing cost up. The larger size also drives the printing cost up.

However, I hate squinting when reading a recipe and when you are cooking I think it is better to have a larger book to work from.

If by chance, you have a recipe that is not in this book and would like to share it with me, my contact info is listed in the back of this book.

I love cooking and I think cooking should be FUN.

While I think it is important to eat "healthy" I think the recipes in this book are a nice step off the usual path.

I hope you enjoy these recipes as much as I have enjoying finding them, making them and compiling them for you.

Sincerely,

Diana

Table of Contents

Additional Books by Diana Loera 3

Introduction 4

Coca Cola Throughout the Years – Photos from the 1920's to 1950's 9

Fast & Easy Coca Cola® Chicken Breasts 16

Easy Five Ingredient Coca Cola® Chicken 17

Garlic & Onion Coca Cola® Chicken 18

Coca-Cola®-Brined Fried Chicken 19

Coca Cola® Chicken Wings 21

Coca-Cola® Chicken Stir Fry Recipe 22

Lemon Coke Sticky Chicken Wings 24

Fried Chicken Marinated in Coca Cola® 26

Coca-Cola® Drumsticks 27

Slow Cooker French Onion Coca Cola® Chicken Wings 29

Crockpot Coca Cola® Chicken 30

Simple Crockpot BBQ Coca-Cola® Chicken Breasts Recipe 31

Coca-Cola® Chicken Wings 32

Teriyaki Coca Cola® Chicken 33

Coca Cola® Chicken 34

Easy Five Ingredient Coca Cola® Chicken 35

Garlic and Onion Coca Cola® Chicken 36

Indian Coca Cola® Curry Chicken 37

Coca-Cola® Ribs or Chicken Wings Recipe 40

Easy Coca-Cola® Chicken 41

Meatloaf with Coca-Cola ®Glaze 42

Coca Cola® Infused Meatloaf 45

Super Simple Coca Cola® Crock Pot Roast 47

Coca Cola® Chuck Roast Barbecue 48

All Day Crock Pot Slow Cooked Coca Cola® Roast 50

Simple Coca Cola® Roast Beef 51

Coca Cola® Beef Brisket 52

Coca Cola®- Marinated Flank Steak 53

Coca Cola® Shredded Beef Tacos Mexican Style 54

Coca Cola® Burgers	56
Super Simple Coca Cola® Roast	57
Coca Cola® Chuck Roast Barbecue	58
All Day Slow Cooked Coca Cola® Roast	60
3 ingredient Super Simple Coca Cola® Baked Roast Beef	61
Coca Cola® Hungarian Goulash	62
Braised Coca Cola® Sausage & Onions	64
Coca-Cola® Roast Recipe	65
Russian Beef Stroganoff with Coca-Cola®	66
Coca Cola® Basted Ham	68
Coca Cola® Marinated Pork Roast	69
Coca-Cola®-Braised Sausage and Onions	70
UK Glazed Coca Cola® Gammon (Ham)	71
Coca Cola® Gammon (Ham) with Maple & Mustard Glaze	73
Coca Cola® Brown Sugar and Mustard Glazed Bone-in Ham	75
Crock Pot Coca Cola® Ham	77
Monster® Infused Pulled Pork with Coca-Cola® BBQ Sauce	78
Coca-Cola® Glazed Ham with Brown Sugar & Dijon	81
Coca Cola® Glazed Baby Back Ribs	82
Coca Cola® Basted Ham	84
Coca Cola® Marinated Pork Roast	85
Chinese Spare Ribs with Coca Cola® and Soy Sauce	87
Coca Cola Roast Turkey	88
Bourbon and Coca Cola® Marinated Turkey	89
Coca-Cola® Moroccan Turkey with Vegetables	91
Coca-Cola® Basted Turkey Breast	93
Coca Cola® French Onion Soup	94
Coca Cola® Tres Leches Cake	95
Coca Cola® Cake	97
Coca Cola® Carrot Cake	98
Cracker Barrel Copycat Coca Cola® Cake	100
Easy Coca Cola® Cake Recipe	102
Cracker Barrel Copycat Double Chocolate Coca Cola® Cake	104

- Vegan Coca Cola® Cake with Fudgy Frosting 106
- Coca-Cola® Cupcakes 108
- Coca-Cola® Cupcakes with Salted Peanut Butter Frosting 110
- UK Version Coca-Cola® Cake 112
- Coca-Cola® Poke Cake 114
- Coca-Cola® Cake Version 3 116
- Coca Cola® Carrot Cake 118
- Coca-Cola® Cake Recipe 120
- Coca-Cola® Cake Frosting 121
- Bing Cherry Jello Mold with Coca Cola® 122
- Cherry Coke Salad 123
- Coca Cola® and Cherry Jello Salad 124
- Coca Cola® Brownies 125
- Out of this World Coca Cola® Brownies.. 127
- Coca-Cola® Jello Salad with Cherries 128
- Bing Cherry Jello Mold with Coca Cola® 129
- Diet Coke 'Almost Brownies' Recipe 130
- Cherry Coke Salad 131

Coca Cola Throughout the Years – Photos from the 1920's to 1950's

Following are a few Coca Cola themed images that I came across while compiling this book and thought that others may enjoy.

Title: Steiner Plastics, Oyster Bay. Coca Cola sign

Creator(s): Gottscho-Schleisner, Inc., photographer

Related Names: Corydon M. Johnson Co. , client

Date Created/Published: 1953 Apr. 29.

Title: Vintage Coca-Cola sign on an outside wall of a grocery store in Oakville, north of Napa in California's Napa Valley

Creator(s): Highsmith, Carol M., 1946-, photographer Date Created/Published: 2012.

Title: [Woman seated at a soda fountain table is pouring alcohol into a cup from a cane, during Prohibition; with a large Coca-Cola advertisement on the wall], 2/13/22

Date Created/Published: [19]22 February 13.

Title: Detroit, Michigan. Girls playing cards and drinking coca cola

Creator(s): Siegel, Arthur S., photographer

Date Created/Published: 1941 Summer.

Title: Noah Booher stopping for a Coca-Cola and water for the radiator on U.S. Highway Route no. 11, Virginia

Creator(s): Vachon, John, 1914-1975, photographer

Date Created/Published: 1943 Mar.

Title: Coca-Cola shack in Alabama

Creator(s): Evans, Walker, 1903-1975, photographer

Date Created/Published: 1935 Dec.

Title: Cowboy buying a Coca-Cola, polo match, Abilene, Texas

Creator(s): Lee, Russell, 1903-1986, photographer

Date Created/Published: 1939 May.

Fast & Easy Coca Cola® Chicken Breasts

Cooking Time: 30 min

Ingredients

1/2 cup chopped onion

1 tablespoon oil

4 boneless chicken breasts

1 (12 ounce) can Cola®

1 cup ketchup

1/8 teaspoon garlic powder

1/8 teaspoon pepper

1/8 teaspoon salt

4 1/2 teaspoons cornstarch

3 tablespoons cold water

Instructions

1. Sauté onion in oil until tender.

2. Add chicken and brown lightly.

3. Add ketchup, Coca Cola®, garlic powder, salt and pepper.

4. Cover and simmer over medium heat for 25-30 minutes or until juices run clear. If sauce needs to be thickened, blend cornstarch and cold water.

5. Move chicken from pan to warm plate.

6. Gradually add cornstarch mixture to sauce, simmer until thickened.

7. Add chicken to pan to reheat, if needed.

Easy Five Ingredient Coca Cola® Chicken

Preparation Time: 15 minutes

Cooking Time: 1 hr.

Ingredients

1 large fryer, cut up, or 4 chicken breasts, cut into halves

1/2 teaspoon garlic powder

1 cup ketchup

1 cup Coca-Cola® (not diet)

1 tablespoon Worcestershire sauce

Instructions

1. Wash chicken and dry thoroughly. Season with garlic powder, salt, and pepper.
2. Place in a large frying pan.
3. Combine all other ingredients and pour over chicken.
4. Simmer, covered, for 55–60 minutes. Turn one time. .
5. Remove from stove and serve

Garlic & Onion Coca Cola® Chicken

Ingredients

4 chicken breasts (you can use legs and/or thighs instead)

1 Cup Coca Cola® (room temperature)

2 teaspoons crushed garlic

1 small onion sliced thin

1 tablespoon oil

Instructions

1. Sauté the garlic and onion in a bit of oil until slightly brown and soft
2. Add chicken to the garlic
3. Slowly pour Coca Cola® over the chicken
4. Cover and simmer until tender (about 45-60 minutes)
5. Remove chicken and serve. I like scraping up the garlic and onion sauce remaining and topping the chicken with it.

Coca-Cola®-Brined Fried Chicken

Ingredients

12 chicken thighs or legs (skin on)

Oil for frying

Brining Mixture

1 quart Coca-Cola® (room temperature)

1 tsp Liquid Smoke (optional)

2 1/2 tbsp. Worcestershire sauce

1 tbsp. Tabasco (optional)

2 tbsp. ground black pepper

1 tbsp. coarse salt

Batter:

1 egg

3/4 cup vegetable oil

Dry Mix (well combined):

2 tsp baking powder

1 tbsp. coarse salt

1 tsp ground black pepper

1 tbsp. cayenne pepper (optional)

1 tbsp. onion powder

1 tbsp. garlic powder

2 1/2 cups flour

Instructions

1. Rinse chicken, drain, and set aside.
2. Blend together brining mix until salt dissolves.
3. Place chicken in brine in a large covered bowl and marinate, refrigerated, for 4 hours.
4. Whisk egg well
5. Add oil and 2 1/2 cups water.
6. Add in dry mix, whisking slowly so batter doesn't clump.
7. Place cooking oil in a large covered skillet and heat up carefully.
8. While oil is heating, remove chicken from brine, drain on paper towels and pat dry with paper towel.
9. Dip chicken in batter and place (carefully) in hot oil.
10. Adjust heat, as the chicken will bring the oil temperature down — you want that nice frying sizzle which is usually around 350 degrees.
11. Turn chicken regularly using tongs to prevent burning. After about 5 minutes, lower your heat and continue turning the chicken so it doesn't burn.
12. After about 20 – 30 minutes you can remove a piece, pierce it to the bone and check the color of the juice. If the juices run clear, it's done. Continue cooking as necessary or remove from stove and serve.

Coca Cola® Chicken Wings

Prep Time: 10 minutes

Cook Time: 25 minutes

Total Time: 35 minutes

Ingredients

12 chicken wings

1 Cup Coca-Cola® (room temperature)

1 teaspoon vegetable oil

3 tablespoons onion, finely chopped

1 teaspoon light soy sauce

1 tablespoon ginger sliced

Pinch of salt

Instructions

1. Gently sauté the onions and ginger until soft.
2. Add wings to the warm pan and sauté each side for about 4 minutes until the skin is a nice golden brown
3. Add wings and Cola® to the warm pan
4. Pour the Coca Cola® over the wings in the warm pan
5. Turn the flame down and allow wings to gently simmer in the Cola® mix for about 15 minutes
6. Turn the flame up, add the soy sauce and stir frequently while the sauce thickens.
7. Remove from stove and place on a serving plate.

Coca-Cola® Chicken Stir Fry Recipe

Ingredients:

3 tbsp. sesame oil

2 small chicken breast cut into small bite size chunks

3 tbsp. chili and garlic stir fry paste

1 package 16 ounces frozen Chinese stir fry vegetable mix

3 tbsp. soy sauce

1 lime, juice only

1 cup (250ml) Coca-Cola®

Optional – cashews and chopped green onion for garnish

Directions

1. Heat the oil in a wok until hot and brown the chicken for several minutes.

2. Add chili and garlic paste to the pan. Stir constantly for 4-5 minutes so chicken is coated evenly.

3. You want to ensure your chicken is cooked before proceeding so remove a piece from wok, cut with a knife and ensure juice is clear and there is zero pink. Then proceed.

4. Add frozen vegetables and continue to stir to coat.

5. Pour in soy sauce, lime juice and Coca-Cola®.

6. Bring to the boil and simmer for 3-4 minutes or until the Coca Cola® reduces by a third.

7. Remove from heat and serve over Asian style noodles or Jasmine rice.

8. Optional – garnish with cashews and chopped green onion.

Lemon Coke Sticky Chicken Wings

Ingredients

12 chicken wings thawed

1 cup Coca Cola®

Oil for cooking

Marinade

2 tbsp. Shaoxing wine

2 tbsp. soy sauce

2 cloves garlic, pounded

¼ ground white pepper

¼ tsp salt

1 tbsp. sesame oil

1 tbsp. vegetable oil

2 tbsp. lemon juice

1 tbsp. sugar

Garnish (optional)

Grated lemon zest

Directions

1. Thoroughly mix chicken with all marinade ingredients except sesame oil, in a dish that can hold the wings in a single layer.

2. Drizzle with sesame oil and mix again. Cover and refrigerate 24-48 hours. Turn chicken midway.

3. Drain chicken wings (but save marinade)

4. Bring chicken wings to room temperature

5. Pan-fry in hot vegetable oil till golden brown, in 2 batches if necessary.

6. Remove chicken to a plate. Remove oil from wok.

7. Put coke and marinade in the wok.

8. Cook on high heat till reduced to about one-quarter.

9. Add sugar and lemon juice. Continue reducing till dark and thick. Taste and adjust seasoning if necessary.

10. Add chicken wings and toss till well coated.

11. Remove from wok and place on a serving plate

12. Garnish with lemon zest.

Fried Chicken Marinated in Coca Cola®

Ingredients

6 chicken thighs or legs

1 cup Coca Cola®

1 Tablespoon soy sauce

1 tsp grated ginger

Flour for frying (I prefer to season the flour with salt, pepper, Italian seasoning, dried chopped onion and dried chopped garlic. I then put seasoned flour in a baggy and drop each piece of chicken in one by one to coat.

Frying oil

Direction

1. Put the Coca Cola®, soy sauce and ginger in a plastic bag with the chicken pieces and marinate for 4 to 8 hours in the refrigerator. I usually put the filled plastic bag in to a deep bowl to prevent accidental leakages.
2. Remove chicken from marinade
3. Pat excess moisture with kitchen paper towels and coat the chicken with flour
4. Heat oil in a pan and fry the chicken, starting at medium heat and finishing at high to make them crispy.
5. Drain the oil and put the chicken on serving plates.

Coca-Cola® Drumsticks

Prep time: 8 hours

Cook time: 55 minutes

Total time: 8 hours 55 minutes

Ingredients

4 lbs. chicken legs or thighs

1 cup chicken broth

Marinade

1 cup Coca Cola®

¼ cup diced onion

¼ cup packed brown sugar

4 garlic cloves chopped fine (I prefer to buy the chopped garlic and use it. A small jar is usually a dollar or two depending where you shop. A very large jar is less than $10 at wholesale clubs)

2 tablespoons ketchup

1 tablespoon minced fresh ginger

1 tablespoon yellow mustard

1 tablespoon Worcestershire sauce

1 teaspoon soy sauce

1 teaspoon salt

Instructions

1. Mix together the marinade ingredients in a large bowl or gallon size re-sealable baggie.

2. Add chicken and toss to coat.

3. Marinate in the refrigerator for at least 2 hours, preferably 4 to 8 hours.

4. Preheat oven to 350 degrees.

5. Remove chicken from container and reserve remaining marinade.

6. Bring reserved marinade and chicken broth to a boil in a medium saucepan. Continue to boil for 15-20 minutes.

7. Arrange chicken on a large greased baking sheet and bake for 45-55 minutes, occasionally basting with reserved marinade mixture, until the skin is brown and crisp and juices run clear.

Slow Cooker French Onion Coca Cola® Chicken Wings

Ingredients:

2 ½ lbs. chicken wings

2/3 cup brown sugar

1 (12 ounce) can Coca-Cola®

1 packet French onion dip mix

1 medium onion, chopped

2 tablespoons soy sauce

Salt and pepper, to taste

Green onions, for garnish

Cornstarch, for thickening

Directions:

1. In a mixing bowl, whisk together the brown sugar, Coke, French onion dip mix, onion, soy sauce, salt and pepper.

2. Pour 3/4 of the sauce and the chicken wings into a slow cooker.

3. Refrigerate remaining sauce

4. Cook on low for 8 hours, stirring occasionally, until the chicken wings are fork tender.

5. Warm the remaining sauce on the stove.

6. Add a dash of cornstarch to the remaining 1/4 of the sauce, and whisk to thicken.

7. Remove chicken wings from slow cooker and place on serving plate

8. Pour the sauce over the wings, and garnish with the green onions.

Crockpot Coca Cola® Chicken

This is probably the recipe that got me really hooked on finding Coca Cola® recipes several years ago. My sister in law gave me the recipe. I usually make it with the optional lemon slices but you can choose not to do so.

Prep Time: 5-10 minutes

Cook Time: 6 to 8 hours

Total Time: 6 hours 5 minutes to 8 hours 10 minutes

INGREDIENTS

1 whole chicken, about 3-4 pounds

1 cup ketchup

1 large onion, thinly sliced

1 Cup Coca Cola®

1 lemon thinly sliced

PREPARATION

1. Wash and pat chicken dry. Salt and pepper to taste.
2. Put chicken in your crock pot with a tiny bit of water on the bottom
3. Mix together Coca Cola® and ketchup and slowly pour over chicken
4. Top with the sliced onions
5. Top with the lemon slices (this is optional but it does add a nice flavor)
6. Cover and cook on LOW 6 to 8 hours until thoroughly cooked.
7. Remove from crock pot and serve

Simple Crockpot BBQ Coca-Cola® Chicken Breasts Recipe

Ingredients

4 – 5 Boneless Skinless Chicken Breasts (thawed if using frozen chicken)

One 18 oz. Bottle Sweet Baby Ray's Barbeque Sauce

1 cup Coca-Cola®

1 small onion sliced

Directions

1. Cook chicken and onion in crockpot on high for 3 hours in crock pot (add a little water or chicken broth to the crock pot before adding the chicken)

2. After 3 hours, drain juices from crockpot

3. Mix together BBQ Sauce and Coca-Cola®

4. Pour mixture over chicken and onions, and cook on high in the covered crockpot for 30 more minutes

Note- this is a fast and easy recipe that you can usually whip up with items in your pantry and freezer

Coca-Cola® Chicken Wings

Ingredients

2 pounds chicken wings

1/4 cup soy sauce

2 tablespoons canola oil

2 tablespoons dry sherry or Chinese rice wine

3/4 cup Coca-Cola® (not diet or flavored)

1 small onion, chopped

6 green onions, chopped

A few pinches of freshly ground black pepper

Sesame oil

Instructions

1. Put the chicken wings in a large bowl and pour half of the soy sauce on top.

2. Turn the wings so they are well-coated and allow them to marinate for 10 to 15 minutes at room temperature.

3. Heat a wok or large deep skillet over medium heat and add sesame oil

4. Cook the onions until soft.

5. Increase the flame and add wings

6. Sear the chicken wings until they are golden brown on each side but not cooked through, about 3 minutes each side.

7. Pour in the other half of the soy sauce, the sherry, and the Coke and bring the liquid to a simmer.

8. Simmer the wings uncovered for 15 to 20 minutes, until the liquid is reduced to a glaze.

9. Season the chicken with black pepper. Transfer the chicken to a plate, garnish with chopped green onions, and serve.

Teriyaki Coca Cola® Chicken

Ingredients:

500g /18 oz. (About 4 pieces) chicken thigh fillets, diced

4 cloves of garlic, grated

1 inch thick ginger, grated

1 cup Pepsi/Coca-Cola® (it doesn't have to be flat)

Light soy sauce to taste

White pepper

Sesame oil (about half a tablespoon)

1 tbsp. sesame seeds, toasted

Methods:

1. Peel ginger and garlic. Grate them onto a bowl and set aside.
2. Dice the chicken thighs.
3. Heat a stir fry pan on medium flame, and dry toast 1 tbsp. of sesame seeds until browned lightly. Remove from pan and place on a flat plate to cool.
4. Add grated ginger, garlic and sesame oil over medium flame until it sizzles.
5. Add chicken and white pepper. Stir to combine the chicken with the ginger-garlic mixture. Brown the chicken over medium heat.
6. Remove the chicken and 1 cup of Pepsi. Allow the mixture to cook on high heat until thickens (above half the original amount).
7. Add chicken and season with soy sauce to taste. Over low heat, simmer the chicken until the sauce thickens a little more.
8. Sprinkle the toasted sesame seeds just before serving. Best eaten with steamed rice.

Coca Cola® Chicken

Cooking Time: 30 min

Ingredients

1/2 cup chopped onion

1 tablespoon oil

4 boneless chicken breasts

1 (12 ounce) can Cola®

1 cup ketchup

1/8 teaspoon garlic powder

1/8 teaspoon pepper

1/8 teaspoon salt

4 1/2 teaspoons cornstarch

3 tablespoons cold water

Instructions

1. Sauté onion in oil until tender.

2. Add chicken and brown lightly.

3. Add ketchup, Cola®, garlic powder, salt and pepper.

4. Cover and simmer over medium heat for 25-30 minutes or until juices run clear. If sauce needs to be thickened, blend cornstarch and cold water.

5. Move chicken from pan to warm plate.

6. Gradually add cornstarch mixture to sauce, simmer until thickened.

7. Add chicken to pan to reheat, if needed.

Easy Five Ingredient Coca Cola® Chicken

Serves: 4

Preparation Time: 15 min

Cooking Time: 1 hr.

Ingredients

4 chicken breasts, cut in halves

1/2 teaspoon garlic powder

1 cup ketchup

1 cup Coca-Cola®

1 tablespoon Worcestershire sauce

Oil to cook

Instructions

1. Season chicken with garlic powder, salt, and pepper.
2. Place in a large heated oiled frying pan.
3. Combine all other ingredients and pour over chicken.
4. Simmer, covered, for about 55–60 minutes.

Garlic and Onion Coca Cola® Chicken

Ingredients

6 chicken legs or thighs

1 teaspoon crushed garlic

1 teaspoon soy sauce

1 Cup Coca Cola®

1 small onion diced

Oil for cooking

Instructions

1. Sauté garlic and onion in a bit of oil until soft
2. Add chicken to garlic and onions and sauté chicken for about 10 minutes
3. Add Cola®
4. Cover and simmer till tender and chicken is thoroughly cooked.
5. Add soy sauce
6. Remove from stove and place on serving dishes
7. I like to top chicken with any leftover Cola® sauce in the pan

Indian Coca Cola® Curry Chicken

TOTAL TIME: 1 hr. 20 min

Prep Time: 15 min

Cook Time: 1 hr. 5 min

Ingredients

2 ½ pounds cut-up chicken or chicken breasts

3 tablespoons butter or margarine

1 tart apple

1 medium onion

1 tablespoon curry powder

⅓ Cup golden raisins

1 cup chicken broth

½ cups Coca-Cola®

3 ½ tablespoons flour

1 cup coffee cream or undiluted evaporated milk

1 teaspoon salt

Pinch of white pepper

1 cup celery tops

Preparation

1. Rinse chicken and cook in boiling salted water with a few celery tops.

2. Cover and simmer about 1 hour or until fork-tender. Drain, saving strained broth.

3. Remove chicken from bones and cut into 1/2-inch pieces to measure about 2 1/2 cups.

4. Melt butter in skillet.

5. Add peeled and diced apple, thinly sliced onion and curry powder, and sauté for 5 minutes, blending well.

6. Stir in raisins, 1 cup of the reserved chicken broth and Coca-Cola®.

7. Mix flour with the cream, stirring until smooth.

8. Add this mixture with the salt and pepper to the onion-apple mixture.

9. Stir and cook over low heat until thick and creamy.

10. Add chicken and place in refrigerator in a covered bowl overnight.

11. Reheat the next day

12. Serve over jasmine rice

Coca-Cola® Ribs or Chicken Wings Recipe

TOTAL TIME: 2 hr. 15 min

Prep Time: 15 min

Cook Time: 2 hr.

Ingredients

1 cup brown sugar

1 can Coca-Cola®

2 medium onions, chopped

2 cloves garlic, minced

2 tablespoons soy sauce

Salt and pepper to taste

2.5 pounds chicken wings or ribs

Directions

1. In a large casserole, combine the brown sugar, Coca-Cola®, onions, garlic, soy sauce, salt and pepper.
2. Stir well until thoroughly mixed
3. Place chicken wings or ribs in sauce mixture.
4. Bake at 350 degrees for 2 hours.
5. Remove from oven and place on serving dishes.

Easy Coca-Cola® Chicken

TOTAL TIME: 1 hr. 5 min

Prep Time: 5 min

Cook Time: 1 hr.

Ingredients

1 cut-up chicken

1 can Coca-Cola®

1 cup ketchup

1 chopped onion

Oil to cook

Preparation

1. Heat deep skillet on stove with oil in pan
2. Add chopped onion and lightly sauté for 5 minutes
3. Carefully add chicken pieces into heated frying pan
4. Combine Coca-Cola® and ketchup and pour over meat.
5. Cover and let simmer (stirring occasionally) for about 60 minutes
6. Remove from stove and carefully place on serving dish
7. I like to top chicken with any remaining sauce in skillet

Meatloaf with Coca-Cola ®Glaze

Meat Loaf

1 lb. ground turkey

1 lb. ground beef

2 cups bread crumbs

1/2 large white onion finely chopped

1 yellow bell pepper finely chopped

1 clove garlic finely minced

1 tbsp. balsamic vinegar

1 tbsp. Worcestershire sauce

1 1/2 tbsp. salt

1 tbsp. ground black pepper

1 tbsp. Cajun seasoning

2 large eggs beaten

1 tbsp. butter unsalted

1. Preheat oven to 350 degrees.
2. In a food processor add enough fresh bread to make 2 cups of crumbs.
3. Then in a hot pan sauté the yellow bell pepper and onion in butter until translucent.
4. In a large bowl combine all ingredients and with your hands mix it together.
5. Mix the meat and ingredients until it is nicely blended
6. Move the meat to a lightly greased cookie sheet and hand mold the meat into a loaf.
7. Cover the meat in a heavy coat of the Coca-Cola® Glaze and cook in the oven until the middle of the meat reads 160 degrees on a thermometer.
8. When the meat reaches the correct temperature, remove from oven and lightly cover with foil to rest for 5 to 10 minutes.
9. If you want more of a glaze crust, add more glaze and place under the broiler till crust is formed, being careful not to burn.
10. Slice and serve.

Glaze recipe follows

Coca-Cola® Glaze

10 ounces Coca-Cola®

1 tbsp. spicy mustard

1/2 cup ketchup

1 clove garlic minced

On medium-high, use a sauce pan and reduce the Coca Cola®, after 10 – 15 min of reducing add the ketchup, mustard and garlic.

Lower the temp to a simmer and allow to continue for an additional 15 min.

The flavors will become rich and sweet, and the texture will be almost syrup like.

Remove warm and cover meat loaf.

Coca Cola® Infused Meatloaf

1 3/4 cup bread crumbs, fresh

1 large egg (well beaten)

1/2 c Coca-Cola®

3 Tbsp. ketchup

1 Tbsp. yellow mustard

1 tsp salt

1/2 tsp ground black pepper

1/8 tsp ground red pepper

1 tsp dry basil leaves (crushed)

1/3 c fresh parsley (minced)

1 medium onion (minced)

2 lb ground beef

<u>Meatloaf Topping-</u>

1 small can tomato paste

Directions

1 In a large bowl put the egg, Coca Cola®, ketchup, mustard and bread crumbs and mix together well. Add spices, fresh parsley and onion, mixing well. Add the ground beef and mix together well.

2 Put into a loaf pan (9x5 inches). Bake at 350 degrees for 55 to 75 minutes. Remove from oven and let rest on counter or stove top about 10 minutes before cutting.

3 Halfway through cooking, quickly spread the tomato paste over the meatloaf with a knife. Return to oven to finish baking.

Super Simple Coca Cola® Crock Pot Roast

Cooking Time: 8 hours

Ingredients

Any kind of roast (3 to 4 lbs.)

1 package onion soup mix

1 can Coca Cola®

Instructions

1. Place roast in crock pot (I always add a tiny bit of water to bottom)
2. Pierce the roast several times with a knife or fork
3. Slowly pour Coca Cola® over the roast
4. Shake the packet of onion soup mix before opening
5. Open the packet and then slowly top the roast with it
6. Cook on medium about 8 hours or until roast is tender

Coca Cola® Chuck Roast Barbecue

Cooking Time: 9 hours

Ingredients

2 1/2 pounds boneless chuck roast

2 onions, chopped

12 ounces can Coca Cola®

1/3 cup Worcestershire sauce

1 1/2 tablespoon apple cider vinegar or white vinegar

1 1/2 teaspoon beef bouillon granules

3/4 teaspoon dry mustard or regular mustard

3/4 teaspoon chili powder

1/4 to 1/2 teaspoon ground red pepper

3 cloves garlic or garlic powder

1 cup ketchup

1 tablespoon butter or margarine

Buns   (I prefer the onion buns)

Instructions

1. Place roast in 3 1/2-4-quart cup slow cooker.

2. Add onion.

3. Combine Cola®, Worcestershire sauce, vinegar or bouillon granules, mustard, chili powder, red pepper and garlic.   This is your Sauce.

4. Save 1 cup Sauce, cover and refrigerate.

5. Pour remaining Sauce over roast.

6. Cover and cook on Medium about 8 hours or until tender

7. Remove from crock pot and save any "juice" left in crock pot.

8. You should be able to shred meat with a fork when it is ready. I do this step in a large bowl.

9. Combine reserved sauce, ketchup and butter in saucepan; cook over med. heat stirring constantly, until heated through.

10. Add in the leftover "juice" from crock pot and stir together

11. Pour over the shredded roast and gently mix

12. Serve on onion buns or your choice of hearty buns

All Day Crock Pot Slow Cooked Coca Cola® Roast

Ingredients

1 3 to 4 lb. beef roast

1 envelope dry onion soup mix

1 can Coca Cola®

Red potatoes washed and halved

1 8 ounce package baby carrots, washed

Instructions

1. Place roast in crock pot
2. Add potatoes and carrots
3. Pierce roast numerous times with knife or fork
4. Slowly pour soda over the roast
5. Shake the envelope of dry onion soup mix well before opening
6. Open dry soup mix packet and slowly sprinkle over roast, carrots and potatoes
7. Cook on medium approximately 8 hours until roast is tender
8. Carefully remove roast and vegetables from crock pot and serve

Simple Coca Cola® Roast Beef

Cooking Time: 4 hr.

Ingredients

1 (3 to 4 pound) beef roast (sirloin tip, round, or boneless chuck)

1 can Coca-Cola®

1 package onion soup mix

Instructions

1. Place unseasoned roast in baking pan.
2. Sprinkle onion soup mix on top.
3. Pour on the Coca-Cola®.
4. Cover tightly with aluminum foil.
5. Bake in oven at 300 degrees F for 3 to 4 hours or until tender.

Coca Cola® Beef Brisket

Cooking Time: 6 to 8 hours

Ingredients

1 Beef Brisket or Roast – 3 to 4 lbs.

1 cup double strength coffee brewed

1 cup hot water with

1 Beef bouillon cube dissolved in hot water above

10 ounces Coca Cola®

1/4 cup Worcestershire

4 tablespoons brown sugar

2 tablespoons liquid smoke

Instructions

1. Place brisket in crock pot.
2. Pour the cup of hot water with dissolved beef bouillon cube in it over the meat
3. Mix the hot coffee and room temperature Coca Cola® together
4. Add in the Worcestershire, brown sugar and liquid smoke
5. Slowly pour the liquid mixture above over the meat
6. Cook on high for 6 to 8 hours
7. I like to baste the brisket sporadically with juices in the crock pot while the brisket is cooking.

Coca Cola®- Marinated Flank Steak

Ingredients

2 pounds beef flank steak

1 cup bottled teriyaki sauce

1 cup Coca Cola®

1 onion, diced

1 clove garlic, chopped

2 tablespoons red wine vinegar

1 teaspoon vegetable oil

2 tablespoons hot sauce

Salt and pepper

Preparation

With a sharp knife, lightly score both sides of steak in a crisscross pattern.

Place steak in a large Ziploc bag.

In a medium bowl, combine teriyaki sauce, Coca Cola®, onion, garlic, vinegar, oil and hot sauce, whisking well to combine.

Reserve 1/2 cup of marinade. Pour remaining marinade over steak in Ziploc bag, seal bag and turn over a few times to thoroughly coat.

Refrigerate for 3-6 hours.

Preheat broiler and place a rack 3 inches from heat source.

Let steak and marinade sit at room temperature for 15 minutes.

Remove steak from bag; discard excess marinade (not reserved marinade, just marinade in this bag)

Season steak on both sides with salt and pepper.

Place steak on a broiler pan and broil for 6 minutes. Turn steak, brush with reserved marinade and broil for 6 minutes longer (for medium rare) or a bit longer if you like it cooked more.

Remove steak to a cutting board. Make a tent with foil to keep warm and allow to rest for 10 minutes.

Carve steak into thin slices and serve.

Coca Cola® Shredded Beef Tacos Mexican Style

Note- these peppers will add some serious "heat" to this dish. If you are not used to spicy food, reduce or eliminate the peppers. Be very careful when handling the peppers also.

Ingredients

3 to 4 lbs. chuck roast, quartered

2 medium dried Ancho peppers

1 large dried Guajillo peppers

2 tablespoons canola oil, divided

1/4 cup finely chopped red onion

2 large garlic cloves, sliced

1/2 teaspoon cumin seeds

1 cup canned diced tomatoes

1 teaspoon dried Mexican oregano*

2 teaspoons kosher salt, divided

1 dried bay leaf

1 1/2 cups Mexican Coca-Cola®* (cane-sugar sweetened) or USA Coca Cola® (not diet)

12 to 24 warm corn tortillas (6-in. size)

Possible toppings - chopped avocado, red onion, and cilantro; thinly sliced pickled jalapeños; and crema Mexicana* or regular sour cream

Preparation

1. Remove stem and seeds from chili peppers, and chop finely.
2. Heat 1 tbsp. oil in a heavy medium saucepan over medium heat.
3. Sauté onion and garlic until softened, 1 to 2 minutes.
4. Add peppers and cook, stirring, until fragrant, 1 to 2 minutes.
5. Add 1 1/2 cups water, the cumin, tomatoes, oregano, and 1 tsp. salt.
6. Bring to a boil, then reduce heat and simmer, covered, until peppers are softened, about 10 minutes.
7. Purée sauce in a blender until very smooth.
8. Season beef with the remaining tsp. salt.
9. Heat the remaining tbsp. oil in a 5- to 6-qt. pot over medium-high heat.
10. Brown beef, turning occasionally, 10 to 14 minutes. Discard fat, if any.

11. Pour sauce into pot, add bay leaf and Coca Cola®
12. Cover, reduce heat, and simmer until beef is very tender in approximately 3 to 4 hours.
13. Using a slotted spoon, transfer beef to a plate.
14. Let cool slightly, then tear into shreds, discarding any fat or gristle.
15. Boil sauce over medium-high heat, stirring occasionally, until slightly thickened and reduced to about 3 cups, 10 to 30 minutes.
16. Stir in beef and heat a few minutes until hot.
17. Remove bay leaf.
18. Make tacos and serve

*Found in the Ethnic foods aisle or spice aisle of grocery store or at a Latino market.

Coca Cola® Burgers

Prep Time: 10 minutes

Cook Time: 15 minutes

Total Time: 25 minutes

Ingredients

1 ½ lbs. ground beef or ground chuck

1 egg

1/2 cup Coca-Cola®

1/2 cup crushed saltine crackers

6 Tbsp. French salad dressing (you will be dividing)

2 Tbsp. grated Parmesan cheese

Instructions:

1. Preheat grill until it reaches about 400 degrees.
2. In a bowl, mix together the egg, 1/4 cup of Coca-Cola®, saltines, 2 tablespoons of French dressing, and Parmesan cheese.
3. Mix in the ground beef.
4. Form into 6 patties.
5. Pour the remaining Coca-Cola® and dressing into a small bowl, and mix well.
6. Place burger patties on grill, brushing with the Coca-Cola® during grilling.
7. Grill for about 6 minutes on each side, or until they are cooked as you like them.
8. Remove from grill and serve

Super Simple Coca Cola® Roast

Cooking Time: 6 to 8 hours

Ingredients

½ cup water

3 – 4 lbs. Roast

2 Pinches dried Italian seasonings

1 package onion soup mix

1 can Coca Cola®

Instructions

1. Put water in bottom of crock pot and turn on high
2. Add 1 pinch Italian seasoning to water
3. Place roast in crock pot
4. Poke holes in roast with a sharp knife
5. Slowly pour Coca Cola® all over roast
6. Sprinkle 1 pinch Italian seasoning over roast
7. Sprinkle onion soup mix over the roast
8. Cover and cook until tender.
9. If I'm home during the day, I like to cook on high 4 ½ -5 hours and then reduce to medium heat for the remaining time.

Coca Cola® Chuck Roast Barbecue

Cooking Time: 6 ½ to 9 ½ hours

Ingredients

2 1/2 pounds boneless chuck roast

1 onion, chopped

12 ounces can Coca Cola®

1/3 cup Worcestershire sauce

1 1/2 tablespoon apple cider vinegar

1 1/2 teaspoon beef bouillon granules

3/4 teaspoon dry mustard or regular mustard

3/4 teaspoon chili powder

1/4 to 1/2 teaspoon ground red pepper

2 cloves garlic or garlic powder

1 cup ketchup

1 tablespoon butter or margarine

Buns

Instructions

1. Place roast in slow cooker.
2. Add onion
3. Combine Cola®, Worcestershire sauce, vinegar or bouillon granules, mustard, chili powder, red pepper and garlic.
4. Save 1 cup Sauce, cover and refrigerate.
5. Pour remaining sauce over roast.

6. Cover and cook high 6 hours, or low 9 hours until tender.

7. Shred meat with a fork.

8. Combine reserved sauce, ketchup and butter in saucepan; cook over med. heat stirring constantly, until heated through.

9. Pour over shredded meat and stir thoroughly

10. Allow to cook on low for 30 minutes

11. Place roast on buns and serve

All Day Slow Cooked Coca Cola® Roast

Ingredients

1 beef roast 3 to 4 lbs.

1 envelope dry onion soup mix

1 can Coca Cola®

Red potatoes, quartered

Carrots, sliced

1 can of corn, drained

Instructions

1. Place roast in slow cooker.
2. Add vegetables around roast
3. Pour Coca Cola® over roast
4. Pour onion soup mix over roast
5. Cook for 6=9 hours until tender
6. Remove from slow cooker and serve

3 ingredient Super Simple Coca Cola® Baked Roast Beef

Cooking Time: 4 hr.

Ingredients

1 (3 to 4 pound) beef roast (sirloin tip, round, or boneless chuck)

1 can Coca-Cola®

1 package onion soup mix

Instructions

1. Place unseasoned roast in baking pan.
2. Sprinkle onion soup mix on top.
3. Pour on the Coca-Cola®.
4. Cover tightly with aluminum foil.
5. Bake in oven at 300 degrees Fahrenheit for 3 to 4 hours or until tender.

Coca Cola® Hungarian Goulash

TOTAL TIME: 1 hr. 25 min

Prep Time: 10 min

Cook Time: 1 hr. 15 min

Ingredients

3 pounds lean beef chuck

2 tablespoons butter

1 cup chopped onions

1 clove garlic, minced

1 tablespoon paprika

2.5 teaspoons salt

½ teaspoon caraway seeds

1 cup Coca-Cola ®

¼ cups dry red wine

4 ripe tomatoes, peeled

3 tablespoons flour

6 cups hot cooked noodles or macaroni

Preparation

1. Cut beef into 1-inch cubes, discarding bone and fat.
2. In a Dutch oven, melt margarine and add meat, stirring to brown on all sides.
3. Remove meat cubes as they brown.
4. Sauté onions and garlic in the drippings until they are soft.
5. Stir in paprika, salt and caraway seeds; cook 1 minute.
6. Stir in meat, Coca-Cola®, wine, and peeled, cut-up tomatoes.

7. Cover tightly; simmer about 1 1/4 hours or until meat is fork-tender.
8. Blend flour with a little water to make a smooth paste; stir into goulash.
9. Stir and cook 3 to 5 minutes until gravy is thickened.
10. Mix in hot noodles and serve.
10. Makes 6 cups goulash or 8 servings.

Braised Coca Cola® Sausage & Onions

Ingredients:

1 tbsp. extra virgin olive oil

2 sweet onions, sliced thin

1 cup Coca Cola®

2 tbsp. honey

1 pinch dried thyme

4 – 8 fully cooked sausages (I like the chicken and apple ones best but you may wish to try other kinds)

Preparation:

1. Preheat oven to 375 degrees F.
2. Heat the olive oil in your oven safe Dutch oven over medium heat.
3. Add onions and season with salt and pepper.
4. Cook 3 to 5 minutes, until tender.
5. Add the Cola®, honey, and thyme, stirring to coat the onions and cook for another 5 minutes.
6. Place the sausages over top of the onions and place in the oven to cook for 20 to 25 minutes.
7. Using oven mitts, carefully remove from oven.
8. Serve sausages and onions with mashed sweet potatoes.

Note – if you do not have a Dutch oven, you can cook everything but the sausages in a skillet. Transfer to your baking pan, add sausages and place in oven. Then follow instructions from Number 6 above.

Coca-Cola® Roast Recipe

TOTAL TIME: 2 hours 10 minutes

Prep Time: 10 minutes

Cook Time: 2 hours

Ingredients

1 beef roast 93 to 4 lbs0

1 can Coca-Cola®

2 cans cream of mushroom soup

1 package of dry onion soup mix

Preparation

1. Place roast in pan.

2. Mix all other ingredients together and pour over roast.

3. Cover tightly with foil and bake at 325 degrees for about 3-4 hours.

Russian Beef Stroganoff with Coca-Cola®

Ingredients

1/2 cup Onion; finely chopped

1/4 cup Water

1 cup Sour cream

1 clove Garlic; minced

1 tbsp. Worcestershire Sauce

2 tbsp. Parsley; minced

2 tbsp. cooking oil

1 small can Mushrooms; with liquid

3 tbsp. Flour

1/2 c Coca Cola®

1 1/2 lb. Chuck steak; or Round Steak, boneless

1 pinch Salt

Noodles; or mashed potatoes or rice, cooked and hot

1/2 c Water

2 tbsp. Flour

Directions

1. Cut beef into 1/2-inch strips; put in a plastic bag with 3 tablespoons of flour and the salt. Shake until the meat is evenly coated.

2. In a heavy skillet or Dutch oven, heat oil, add the meat strips and brown slowly, stirring often.

3. Add onion, garlic, Coca-Cola®, and 1/4 cup of water; mix well. Cover and simmer 30 to 45 minutes or until the meat is fork-tender.

4. In a bowl, mix the 2 tablespoons of flour with the 1/2 cup of water until smooth.

5. Stir into the meat along with the Worcestershire sauce and the undrained mushrooms.

6. Stir and cook until thickened, 2 to 3 minutes. (If making ahead for reheating later, do not add the sour cream now. Reheat, then complete the recipe directions.)

7. Stir in the sour cream and heat gently just until the gravy simmers.
8. Sprinkle with parsley and serve over potatoes, noodles, or rice.

Coca Cola® Basted Ham

Cooking Time: 35 minutes

Ingredients

1 ham

1 1/2 cup brown sugar

2 teaspoons dry mustard

1/2 cup dry fine bread crumbs

12 ounces Coca Cola®

Cloves (to stud the ham with)

Instructions

1. Cook ham accordingly until it reaches an internal temperature of 160 degrees F.
2. When cool enough to handle, pull off skin.
3. Mix brown sugar, mustard and bread crumbs. Coat top of ham with this mixture
4. Score and stud the ham with cloves.
5. Pour Coca-Cola® around ham; cover and bake at 400 degrees F for approximately 35 minutes.
6. Baste with liquid every 15 minutes.
7. Remove from oven. Let ham rest for 15 minutes before carving.

Coca Cola® Marinated Pork Roast

Cooking Time: 3 hours

Ingredients

1/2 cup soy sauce

1/2 cup Coca-Cola®

2 cloves garlic, minced

1 tablespoon dry mustard

1 teaspoon ginger

1 teaspoon thyme, crushed

5 pounds pork loin roast, boned & rolled

Instructions
1. Combine all the ingredients except for the meat, to form a marinade.
2. Place meat into a large "zip-lock" plastic bag which has been set into a deep bowl to steady the meat.
3. Add the marinade and seal the bag.
4. Allow the roast to marinate overnight in the refrigerator.
5. Remove the meat and roast on a rack, in a shallow roasting pan.
6. Preheat oven to 325 degrees F.
7. Roast in oven 2 1/2 - 3 hr. at 325F, or until a meat thermometer registers 175F.
8. Baste occasionally with the marinade during the last hour of roasting.
9. Remove from oven and transfer to serving dishes

Coca-Cola®-Braised Sausage and Onions

Ingredients:

4 chorizo sausages

1 tablespoon extra-virgin olive oil

2 onions, sliced

1 packet French onion dip mix

1 cup sliced mushrooms

1 cup Coca-Cola®

1 tablespoon brown sugar

Fresh parsley

2 cups mashed potatoes (heated)

Directions:
1. In a large Dutch oven, heat the olive oil over medium-high heat.
2. Add the onions and mushrooms, and cook until softened, about 5 minutes.
3. Stir in the French onion dip mix, brown sugar and Cola®.
4. Add the sausages.
5. Reduce the heat to low, and simmer for about 20 minutes or until the liquid has mostly evaporated.
6. Slice the sausages into bite-sized pieces, and place over mashed potatoes with the caramelized onions and mushrooms
7. Garnish with fresh parsley.

UK Glazed Coca Cola® Gammon (Ham)

Ingredients

For the Ham

2 kilograms mild-cure gammon joint

1 onion (peeled and cut in half)

2 litres Coca-Cola®

For the glaze

1 handful of cloves

1 heaped tablespoon black treacle

2 teaspoons English mustard powder

2 tablespoons Demerara sugar

Directions

1. Put the gammon in a pan, skin-side down.
2. Add onion
3. Pour Coca Cola® over gammon
4. Bring to a boil, reduce to a good simmer, put the lid on, though not tightly, and cook for about 2½ hours.
5. Preheat the oven to 240°C/gas mark 9/450ºF.
6. Allow to cool enough to be able to remove skin from ham. Leave a thin layer of fat.
7. Score the fat with a sharp knife to make fairly large diamond shapes, and stud each diamond with a clove.
8. Then carefully spread the treacle over the bark-budded skin, taking care not to dislodge the cloves.
9. Gently pat the mustard and sugar onto the sticky fat.

10. Cook in a foil-lined roasting tin for approximately 10 minutes or until the glaze is burnished and bubbly.
11. Remove from oven and allow to rest 15 minutes before cutting

Coca Cola® Gammon (Ham) with Maple & Mustard Glaze

Ingredients

2kg unsmoked boneless gammon joint

2 liters Coca Cola® (not diet)

1 carrot, chopped

1 onion, peeled and quartered

1 stick celery, chopped

1 cinnamon stick

½ tbsp. peppercorn

1 bay leaf

For the glaze

150ml maple syrup

2 tbsp. wholegrain mustard

2 tbsp. red wine vinegar

Pinch of ground cloves or five-spice

Directions

1. Put the gammon in a large pan and cover with Coca Cola®.
2. Add the carrot, onion, celery, cinnamon stick, peppercorns and bay leaf.
3. Bring to the boil, then turn down to simmer for around 2 1/2 hrs. topping up with boiling water if necessary to keep the gammon fully covered.
4. Carefully pour the liquid away
5. Let the ham cool enough to be able to safely remove the skin
6. Preheat the oven to 190C/170C fan/gas 5.
7. Lift the ham into a roasting tin, then cut away the skin leaving behind an even layer of fat
8. Score the fat all over in a crisscross pattern.
9. Mix the glaze ingredients together.
10. Pour half over the ham and roast for 15 minutes
11. Then pour over the remainder over the ham and return to the oven for another 30 minutes.
12. Baste half way through.

13. Remove from the oven and spoon more glaze over the top.
14. Allow ham to rest for 10 minutes
15. Cut and serve

Coca Cola® Brown Sugar and Mustard Glazed Bone-in Ham

Prep time: 10 min

Cook time: 2 hour 30 min

Ingredients

1 (6 to 8 pound) fully cooked, shank-end half ham

1 to 2 cups light brown sugar, firmly packed

1/2 cup yellow or Dijon mustard

I can sliced pineapple (drained)

Whole cloves (enough to stud ham)

Maraschino cherries

1/2 can of (regular) Coca-Cola®

Instructions

1. Preheat the oven to 350 degrees F.
2. Line a roasting pan that is just large enough for the ham with aluminum foil to help with clean-up. Add another section of aluminum foil for wrapping loosely around the ham.
3. Score the ham into a crosshatch pattern and, if desired, stud the intersections of the crosshatches with whole cloves.
4. Mix 1 cup of the brown sugar and mustard together to form a thick paste and smear it all over the ham. Use 2 cups of his mixture if you like your ham to have a sweeter taste.
5. You can substitute most or all of the mustard with the pineapple juice – if you'd rather or if you don't have mustard.
6. Add pineapple slices and decorate the center of the pineapples with a cherry.
7. Pour the Coca Cola® carefully over and around the ham.
8. Pull the foil up loosely around the ham and bring it together, but remember you will need easy access to the ham for basting so don't crimp the foil too tight.
9. Bake at 350 degrees F for about 18 minutes per pound, or until the center of the ham reaches slightly over 140 degrees F on an instant read thermometer, basting occasionally. Check the instructions on ham package for their recommendations as different companies may give variations on baking.
10. If desired, unwrap the ham and place it under the broiler to brown, with the door ajar, about 5 minutes, watch it carefully.

11. Remove ham to cutting board and allow to cool.
12. Plate the ham and pour the pan drippings all over the top, or to make a pan gravy, plate the ham and drizzle on a few spoons of the drippings.
13. Tent loosely with foil to keep warm. Transfer the remaining pan drippings to a skillet, bring to a boil, stir in 1 to 2 tablespoons of butter to add richness, and let reduce and thicken slightly. Place into a gravy boat for individual pouring when served.

Crock Pot Coca Cola® Ham

Total Time: 8 hours 5 minutes

Prep Time: 5 minutes

Cook Time: 8 hours

Ingredients:

3 -4 lbs. fully cooked boneless ham

1/2 cup packed brown sugar

1 tablespoon mustard

2 (12 ounce) cans Coca-Cola®

Directions:

1. Remove ham from packaging.
2. Lightly score ham in diagonal lines first one way, then crosswise, to form a diamond pattern, being careful not to cut any deeper than about an eighth of an inch. (You can score both sides if you like).
3. Place ham in crock pot
4. Slowly pour two cans of Coca Cola® over the ham.
5. Make a paste of brown sugar and mustard
6. Rub paste into ham on sides that have been lightly scored.
7. Cook on low 7-8 hours.
8. Remove carefully from crockpot.
9. Allow to cool enough to slice
10. Place sliced ham on serving platter

Monster® Infused Pulled Pork with Coca-Cola® BBQ Sauce

Prep Time: 60 minutes

Cook time: 12 hours

Ingredients:

Pulled pork

3 to 4 lbs. pork butt

1 can Monster® Energy drink

12 oz. Barbeque sauce (I like Sweet Baby Ray's brand)

1 can Coca-Cola®

1 medium onion diced

¼ cup Ketchup

3 tbsp. Apple Cider vinegar

2 tbsp. Worcestershire sauce -

Cooking oil to sauté onions

(Optional – ½ cup pineapple diced – sauté it with the onions)

Instructions:

1. Place the pork in the slow cook.
2. Poke holes in pork with knife or fork.
3. Slowly pour Monster drink over pork.
4. Cook pork on low setting 10 to 12 hours
5. About an hour and a half before pork is done cooking, you should make your sauce. You can make beforehand and warm up on stove.
6. Once pork is fork tender, remove it carefully from crock pot.
7. Remove fat and bone then shred pork.
8. Mix the sauce is slowly with your pork. You may not use all the sauce depending on your taste. Start with less as you can always add more.
9. Serve on hearty buns with a side of coleslaw.

Sauce mixture

1. Sauté the onions until slightly caramelized.
2. Slowly add the additional ingredients to your pan
3. Bring the mixture to a very gentle boil
4. Stir thoroughly
5. Lower heat to a low simmer
6. Cover the pan
7. Stir constantly
8. Ideally the sauce will simmer about an hour
9. It will thicken as it simmers so watch it carefully so it doesn't burn

Coca-Cola® Glazed Ham with Brown Sugar & Dijon

Ingredients:

1 10-12 pound bone-in, cured ham (do not use a spiral ham)

1 extra-large (or "turkey size") oven bag (holds 8-25 lbs.)

1/2 cup brown sugar

1/3 cup Dijon mustard

1 large orange, washed and cut into 6 wedges (optional)

1 can Coca-Cola®

Instructions:

1. Trim any excess skin and/or fat from the ham. Using a sharp knife, score the ham in a diamond pattern making 1/4-inch deep slices. Don't fret over getting this perfect - mine certainly wasn't!
2. Place the ham (on its side – not face down) in the oven bag set in a large roasting pan. Roll the sides of the bag down so that the bag is open as you will need to be reaching in yet make sure sides are high
3. Slowly pour 1 can Coca-Cola® over the ham
4. Combine brown sugar and Dijon mustard in a small bowl and stir until thoroughly combined. Rub sugar mixture all over ham.
5. Place orange wedges in the bottom of the bag around the ham.
6. Pull up the bag loosely that the bag isn't touching the ham. Making sure to keep a "loose fit" around the ham, close the bag tightly with the provided tie.
7. Using a small, sharp knife, make three small slits in the top of the bag for ventilation (don't skip this step or the bag will burst wide open and the ham won't be able to self-baste).
8. Move your oven rack just low enough that the bag won't touch the upper elements in your oven then bake at 350 degrees for 2-2.5 hours (2.5-3 hours if using a 13-15 pound ham) or until nicely browned and caramelized.
9. Remove ham from oven and rest, inside the bag, for 30 minutes before serving.

Coca Cola® Glazed Baby Back Ribs

Ingredients

3-4 lbs. baby back ribs

1 cup Coca-Cola® Classic

1/4 cup apple cider vinegar

1 ½ cups firmly packed light brown sugar

¼ to 1 Scotch bonnet chili pepper, chopped (this is a hot pepper so proceed accordingly as it will add some serious heat to your dish)

Coarse salt and freshly ground black pepper

Instructions

1. To make the glaze, in a small saucepan, bring the Coca-Cola®, vinegar, brown sugar, and chili pepper to a boil over high heat;
2. Reduce the heat to medium-low and simmer until syrupy, about 10 minutes.
3. Decrease the heat to low and keep the sauce warm while the ribs cook.
4. Preheat the oven to 325°F.
5. Season both sides of the ribs with salt and pepper.
6. Place the ribs on a broiler pan and bake for 30 minutes, glazing the ribs occasionally with the Coca-Cola® mixture.
7. Turn the ribs over and continue to cook for an additional 30 minutes, glazing occasionally, or until the ribs are tender and the meat is starting to pull away from the bone.
8. Remove from oven and serve.

Coca Cola® Basted Ham

Cooking Time: 35 minutes

Ingredients

1 ham

1 1/2 cup brown sugar

2 teaspoons dry mustard

1/2 cup dry fine bread crumbs

12 ounces Coca Cola®

Cloves to stud the ham

Instructions

1. Cook ham according to package instructions until it reaches an internal temperature of 160 degrees F.
2. When cool enough to handle, pull off skin. Mix brown sugar, mustard and bread crumbs. Coat op of ham.
3. Score and stud with cloves. Pour Coca-Cola® around ham; cover and bake at 400 degrees F for approximately 35 minutes.
4. Baste with liquid every 15 minutes. Let ham set for 30 minutes before carving

Coca Cola® Marinated Pork Roast

Cooking Time: 3 hours

Ingredients

5-6 lbs. pork loin roast, boned and rolled

1/2 cup soy sauce

1/2 cup Coca-Cola®

2 cloves garlic, minced

1 tablespoon dry mustard

1 teaspoon ginger

1 teaspoon thyme, crushed

Instructions

1. Combine all the ingredients in a mixing bowl except for the meat, to form a marinade.
2. Place meat into a large "zip-lock" plastic bag which has been set into a deep bowl to steady the meat.
3. Add the marinade and seal the bag. Allow to marinade overnight in the refrigerator.
4. Occasionally knead the bag to help spread the marinade evenly.
5. Preheat oven to 325F degrees
6. Remove the meat from marinade and roast on a rack, in a shallow roasting pan.
7. Baste occasionally with the marinade especially the last hour of roasting. Total cooking time should be 2-3 hours.

Chinese Spare Ribs with Coca Cola® and Soy Sauce

Ingredients

2 lbs. pork spare ribs

12-oz Coca Cola® at room temperature

2 tbsp. soy sauce

Directions

1.	Wash and cut ribs into sections.

2.	Bring a large pot of water to boil and add the spare ribs. Let them boil for about 10 minutes until scum comes to the surface. Dump everything into a colander and rinse the ribs.

3.	Place the cleaned ribs in a pan on medium heat.

4.	Add 12-oz of Coke and 2 tbsp. soy sauce.

4.	The sauce will eventually reduce and thicken as the ribs cook.

This can take between 20 minutes to 45 minutes depending on your pan and oven

Coca Cola Roast Turkey

Prep Time: 10 minutes

Cooking Time: 4 hours

Ingredients

1 (16 pound) whole turkey - thawed, neck and giblets removed

1/2 cup butter, softened

2 cups Coca Cola®

Salt and ground black pepper to taste

Directions

1. Preheat oven to 325 degrees F (165 degrees C).
2. Wash the turkey well, and pat dry with paper towels.
3. Slather the whole turkey, front and back, with butter. Make sure to butter the wing tips and leg ends.
4. Place the turkey into a roasting pan, and pour the Coca Cola® over the turkey.
5. Sprinkle the whole turkey with salt and black pepper.
6. Roast the turkey for 4 to 5 hours, checking for doneness after 4 hours. Baste the turkey every 30 minutes with the turkey drippings. If the breast skin browns too quickly, cover it with aluminum foil. An instant-read thermometer inserted into the thickest part of the thigh, near the bone should read 180 degrees F (82 degrees C).
7. Remove the turkey from the oven, cover with a doubled sheet of aluminum foil, and allow to rest in a warm area 10 to 15 minutes before slicing.

Bourbon and Coca Cola® Marinated Turkey

Prep Time: 10 minutes

Marinade Time 6 to 8 hours

Cooking Time Approximately 3 to 4 hours depending on turkey size

Ingredients

¾ cup Coca Cola®

½ cup bourbon

⅓ cup fresh lemon juice

⅓ Cup soy sauce

¼ cup chopped green onions

1 tablespoon minced fresh garlic

½ teaspoon crushed red pepper flakes

1 (12 to 14 pound) Fresh or Frozen Whole Turkey, thawed if frozen

(You will also need cooking oil to brush on the turkey)

DIRECTIONS

1. Combine all ingredients except turkey and cooking oil in non-reactive container large enough to hold turkey.
2. Remove turkey from packaging; drain.
3. Remove neck and giblets; refrigerate for another use or discard.
4. Place turkey in marinade. Cover container.
5. Refrigerate 6 to 8 hours, turning turkey over occasionally.
6. Preheat oven to 325°F.
7. Remove turkey from marinade; drain; pat dry.
8. Discard marinade. Place turkey on a flat rack in a shallow roasting pan, 2 to 2-1/2-inches deep.
9. Tuck wings back to hold neck skin in place and stabilize the turkey in the pan and when carving.

10. Brush lightly with vegetable oil or spray with cooking spray to prevent skin from drying
11. . Insert oven-safe thermometer deep into the lower thigh muscle but not touching the bone.
12. Bake 3 to 3-1/2 hours. When the turkey is about 2/3 done, cover the breast and top of thighs lightly with aluminum foil to prevent overcooking.
13. Check for doneness about 30 minutes before end of recommended cooking time.
14. Turkey is done when thigh reaches 180°F and juices run clear.
15. Remove the turkey from the roasting pan.
16. Let rest 15 minutes to allow juices to set before carving.

Coca-Cola® Moroccan Turkey with Vegetables

TOTAL TIME: 5 hr. 30 min

Prep Time: 45 min

Cook Time: 4 hr. 45 min

Ingredients

1 tablespoons olive oil

2 pounds small turkey drumsticks (about 3), patted dry with bottom end removed, if necessary, to fit in slow cooker

1 medium onion, peeled and diced

2 cloves garlic, minced

1 teaspoons ground coriander, plus ½ teaspoon additional at the end

1 teaspoons ground cumin, plus ½ teaspoon additional

1 teaspoon ground cinnamon

1 teaspoon paprika

1 teaspoons ground ginger

2 tablespoons all-purpose flour

1 cup chicken stock, heated

1 cup Coca-Cola® (at room temperature)

Pinch salt and freshly ground black pepper

2 small preserved lemons, flesh and seeds removed, and chopped (about 2 ½ tablespoons)

8 ounces baby carrots

1 medium red bell pepper, seeds and membranes removed, diced

1 medium zucchini, sliced

1 can (16-ounce) can chickpeas, rinsed and drained

3 cups pitted small green olives or cut-up large olives

1 cups chopped mint, plus mint leaves to garnish

Directions

1. Heat the oil in a large skillet over medium-high heat.
2. Add the drumsticks and brown on all sides, turning to cook evenly, about 5 minutes.
3. Transfer to the slow cooker.
4. Add the onion to the skillet and cook until it is starting to color, about 3 minutes.
5. Stir in the garlic and flour, cook for 30 seconds, then stir in the coriander, cumin, cinnamon, paprika and ginger.
6. Add the hot stock and bring the mixture to a boil.
7. Stir in the Coca-Cola® and about 1 teaspoon of salt and black pepper to taste.
8. Scrape into the slow cooker.
9. Cover and cook on high for about 15 minutes until the liquid begins to simmer.
10. Turn the knob to slow/low (depending on your appliance) and cook for about 3 hours.
11. Add the preserved lemons, carrots, bell pepper, zucchini and chickpeas.
12. Cover and cook until the vegetables are tender, about 1 ½ hours.
13. Carefully take the drumsticks out of the pot, remove and discard the skin, bones and tendons.
14. Cut the meat into bite-size pieces and return to the pot.
15. Add the green olives, the remaining ½ teaspoon coriander and cumin and mint.
16. Taste to adjust the seasonings and serve over couscous, garnished with a few mint leaves.

Coca-Cola® Basted Turkey Breast

Total Time: 2 hours 5 minutes

Prep Time: 5 minutes

Cook Time: 2 hours

Ingredients

1 turkey breast, fresh or frozen

1 can Coca-Cola® at room temperature

Directions

1. Put the turkey breast in a roasting pan or Dutch oven.

2. Pour half the can of Coca-Cola® over the turkey.

3. Roast in 325 degree oven, basting often, add more Coca Cola if necessary.

4. When the temperature of the turkey breast reaches 195 degrees on a meat thermometer, or when the turkey timer pops up, the turkey is done.

Coca Cola® French Onion Soup

TOTAL TIME: 45 minutes

Prep Time: 20 minutes

Cook Time: 25 minutes

Ingredients

1/4 cup butter

4 cups thinly sliced onions

2 cans (10.5 oz. each) beef broth (bouillon)

¾ cup Coca-Cola® at room temperature

Pinch of salt

1/2 teaspoons vinegar

Dash of pepper

6 Thick French bread slices

6 teaspoons Grated parmesan cheese

Preparation

1. Melt butter in heavy saucepan; add onions and cook until golden; do not brown.
2. Add undiluted beef broth, 1 soup can of water, Coca-Cola®, salt, vinegar, and pepper.
3. Cover; simmer 20-25 minutes.
4. In a broiler, toast one side of the French bread slices.
5. Turn bread, generously sprinkle with Parmesan cheese and toast until browned.
6. Ladle soup into deep bowls and top with toast, cheese side up.

Makes about 6 cups or 4 servings.

Coca Cola® Tres Leches Cake

Ingredients

1 (15.25 oz.) box Devil's Food Cake Mix

2 1/4 cups Coca Cola® or Cherry Coca Cola® at room temperature (you will be dividing the cola in this recipe)

1 Tbsp. vegetable oil

4 large eggs

1 cup sweetened condensed milk

2/3 cup evaporated milk (1 5oz can)

2/3 cup heavy cream

Sweetened Whipped Cream Frosting:

1 1/3 cups heavy cream

1/4 cup granulated sugar

Cake sprinkles

Directions

1. Preheat oven to 350 degrees.
2. In a large mixing bowl combine cake mix, 1 1/4 cups Coca Cola®, vegetable oil and eggs.
3. Blend ingredients together using an electric mixer, on low speed for 30 seconds, then increase speed to medium and blend mixture for 2 minutes.
4. Pour mixture and evenly spread into a greased 13x9 baking dish.
5. Bake 30-35 minutes or until toothpick inserted into center comes out clean.
6. Remove from oven and allow cake to cool for 5 minutes.
7. Meanwhile, in medium mixing bowl, whisk together sweetened condensed milk, evaporated milk and 2/3 cup heavy cream.
8. Add in 1 cup Coca Cola® and mix until combined.
9. Poke cake every 1/2"-1" with a long tinned fork. Slowly pour Coca Cola® milk mixture evenly over entire cake.
10. Allow cake to rest, uncovered for 30 minutes at room temperature. Cover cake with plastic wrap and refrigerate for 1 hour (or overnight) until cake has cooled completely and the majority of the milk mixture has been absorbed.
11. In a mixing bowl, using an electric mixer, whip heavy cream until soft peaks form.
12. Stir in granulated sugar and whip until stiff peaks form.

13. Spread sweetened whipped cream evenly over cooled cake.
14. Sprinkle frosted cake with optional sprinkles.
15. Serve immediately (note: when cutting and placing on plates using a spatula is the best way to lift cake from pan)
16. Store cake in refrigerator (note that the sweetened whip cream will begin to separate after approximately 3 hours).

Coca Cola® Cake

Cooking Time: 30 minutes

Ingredients

2 cups granulated white sugar

4 tablespoons cocoa

1 stick (1/2 cup) butter (softened)

1/2 cup oil

2 eggs, beaten

1 cup buttermilk

2 cups all-purpose flour

1 teaspoon baking soda

1 teaspoon salt

1 1/2 cup mini marshmallows

1 cup Coca Cola at room temperature

Instructions

1. Cream sugar and butter, add oil, eggs and buttermilk a little at a time.
2. Mix in well - cocoa, flour, soda and salt.
3. Fold in marshmallows and cola.
4. Bake at 350 degrees F for 25 - 30 minutes for 2 layers.

Coca Cola® Carrot Cake

Cooking Time: 50 min

Ingredients

2 cups flour, sifted

1 teaspoon baking soda

1/2 teaspoon salt

2 tablespoons cocoa

3 eggs

1 1/2 cup sugar

1/2 cup vegetable oil

3/4 cup Coca-Cola®

1 1/2 teaspoon vanilla extract

2 1/4 cups raw carrots, grated

1 cup nuts, chopped

1 cup coconut, flaked

3/4 cup sugar

2 teaspoons cocoa

6 tablespoons Coca-Cola®

6 tablespoons butter

1 tablespoon light corn syrup

1/2 teaspoon vanilla

Instructions

1. Mix all the dry ingredients together.
2. Beat the eggs well; add sugar, oil, 3/4 cup Cola®, and vanilla and beat well.
3. Stir in the dry ingredients until smooth, then add the carrots, nuts and coconut. Mix well.

4. Bake in a greased and lightly floured 13 x 9 pan in a preheated 350~F oven for 40-50 minutes, until cake tests done.

5. Remove from oven and prick hot cake all over with a fork, then pour the Coca Cola® syrup slowly, evenly over the top.

6. Serve warm or room temperature with lightly sweetened-vanilla flavored whipped cream.

Coca Cola® Syrup

1. Combine sugar, cocoa, Cola®, butter and corn syrup in saucepan; bring to a boil over medium heat, stirring constantly.

2. Boil, stirring, until thick and syrupy, about 5 minutes.

3. Add vanilla extract.

4. Remove from heat and pour, hot, over hot cake.

Cracker Barrel Copycat Coca Cola® Cake

Cooking Time: 45 minutes

Ingredients

For Cake:

2 cups all-purpose flour

2 cups granulated sugar

3 tablespoons cocoa

1 cup butter or margarine

1/2 cup buttermilk

2 eggs

1 teaspoon baking soda

1 teaspoon vanilla extract

Pinch salt

1 1/2 cup miniature marshmallows

For Frosting:

1/2 cup butter or margarine

3 tablespoons cocoa

6 tablespoons Coca-Cola®

1 box of confectioner's sugar

1 teaspoon vanilla extract

Instructions

For the Cake:

1. Preheat oven to 350 degrees F.

2. Grease and flour a 13 x 9-inch baking pan.

3. Combine dry ingredients in a bowl.

4. Heat butter, cocoa and Coca-Cola® to boil and pour over the flour mixture.

5. Mix well.

6. Add eggs, buttermilk, vanilla extract and marshmallows and blend. The batter will be thin with marshmallows floating on top.

7. Bake for 45 minutes.

8. Remove from oven. Let cool to warm and then frost.

For the Frosting:

1. Boil first three ingredients together in a sauce pan.
2. Remove from the heat and blend in the sugar and vanilla extract.
3. Spread on warm cake.

Easy Coca Cola® Cake Recipe

Ingredients:

1 cup butter

1/3 cup cocoa

1 cup Coca Cola®

2 cups all-purpose flour

1 1/3 cups sugar

1 teaspoon baking soda

2 large eggs

1/2 cup buttermilk

1 teaspoon vanilla extract

1 1/2 cups miniature marshmallows

Cocoa Coca Cola® Icing

1/2 cup butter

1/4 cup cocoa

1/3 cup Cola® soft drink

3 cups powdered sugar

1/2 teaspoon vanilla extract

1 cup chopped pecans

Preparation:

1. Combine first 3 ingredients in a medium saucepan over medium heat, stirring until butter melts.
2. Remove from heat.
3. Combine flour, sugar, and baking soda in a large bowl; stir in butter mixture.
4. Add eggs, and stir until blended.
5. Stir in buttermilk, vanilla, and marshmallows.

6. Pour into a lightly greased 13- x 9-inch baking pan.
7. Bake at 350º for 25 to 30 minutes or until a pick inserted in center comes out clean. Remove from oven; spread Cocoa Coca-Cola® icing over warm cake.

Note: Prepare the icing during the last 10 minutes of baking so it is ready to spoon onto the warm cake.

Cocoa Coca Cola® Icing

1. Combine first 3 ingredients in a medium saucepan over medium heat, stirring until butter melts.
2. Remove from heat; stir in powdered sugar, vanilla, and pecans.
3. Spoon immediately over warm cake.

Cracker Barrel Copycat Double Chocolate Coca Cola® Cake

Ingredients

1 cup Coca Cola®

1/2 cup vegetable oil

1/2 cup (1 stick) salted butter

3 heaping-Tablespoons dark cocoa powder

2 cups granulated sugar

2 cups all-purpose flour

2 large eggs

1/2 cup buttermilk

1 teaspoon baking soda

1 teaspoon vanilla extract

Frosting:

1 stick salted butter

3 tablespoons dark cocoa powder

6 tablespoons milk

1 teaspoon vanilla extract

4 cups powdered sugar

Instructions

1. Preheat oven to 350. Butter and flour a 9x13 pan and set aside.
2. In the large bowl of a mixer, stir together sugar and flour and set aside.
3. In a saucepan, bring Coca Cola®, oil, butter and cocoa to a boil.

4. Pour into the flour mixture and beat on medium low for about a minute.
5. Add eggs, buttermilk, baking soda and vanilla and beat on medium for a minute more.
6. Spread batter into prepared pan and bake for about 30 minutes or until a toothpick inserted in the center comes out clean.
7. Immediately upon removing cake from oven, prepare frosting.
8. In a saucepan over medium heat, bring butter, cocoa powder and milk to JUST boiling.
9. Remove from heat and whisk in powdered sugar and vanilla.
10. Pour over cake and quickly spread.
11. Let cake cool to room temperature, then cover and refrigerate until serving.

Vegan Coca Cola® Cake with Fudgy Frosting

Ingredients

Cake:

2 cups natural sugar

2 cups unbleached all-purpose flour

¼ cup cocoa powder

1 tablespoon baking powder

½ cup dairy-free margarine

½ cup vegetable oil or grape seed oil

1 cup Coca-Cola® (not diet) at room temperature

¾ cup dairy-free buttermilk

1 teaspoon baking soda

1 teaspoon vanilla extract

Frosting:

1 pound powdered confectioner's sugar (plus extra, if needed, to yield the consistency you desire)

½ cup dairy-free margarine

¼ cup cocoa powder

6 tablespoons Coca-Cola® (not diet)

1 teaspoon vanilla extract

1 cup coarsely chopped toasted pecans, optional (omit for nut-free)

Instructions

For the Cake:

1. Preheat your oven to 350ºF and grease a 9 x 13-inch baking pan.

2. In a bowl, combine the sugar, flour, cocoa powder and baking powder.

3. In a 1-quart saucepan, combine the margarine and oil. Bring just to a boil and pour over dry ingredients.

4. Add the Coca Cola® to the batter, and whisk well to combine.

5. Dissolve the baking soda in the vegan buttermilk and add it to the batter along with the vanilla extract. Whisk just until combined. The batter will seem a bit thin.

6. Pour the batter into your prepared pan and bake 35-45 minutes or until a wooden pick inserted in the center of the cake comes out clean.

7. Remove from the oven to a wire rack and frost immediately.

For the Frosting:

1. While the cake bakes, place the confectioner's sugar in a medium bowl.

2. In a 2-quart saucepan, combine the dairy-free margarine, cocoa powder and Coca-Cola®; bring just to a boil.

3. Pour the liquid over the sugar, and whisk to combine until smooth.

4. Add the vanilla extract and pecans (if using), and stir to distribute (or reserve pecan pieces or halves and sprinkle/arrange over the top of the frosted cake).

5. Spread frosting over warm cake. When cool, cut into squares and serve.

Coca-Cola® Cupcakes

Note- I use a pastry bag to do the frosting. You can use a knife instead.

Cupcakes:

2 cups Coca-Cola® at room temperature

1 cup dark unsweetened cocoa powder

1/2 cup (1 stick) unsalted butter, cut into 1-inch pieces

1 1/4 cups granulated sugar

1/2 cup firmly packed dark brown sugar

2 cups all-purpose flour

1 1/4 teaspoons baking soda

1 teaspoon salt

2 large eggs

Whipped Cream Frosting:

1 1/2 cups of heavy whipping cream

4 tablespoons of powdered sugar

1/2 teaspoon of vanilla extract

Maraschino cherries (for topping)

Instructions

1. Preheat the oven to 325 degrees F.
2. Generously spray the inside of the cupcake liners with nonstick cooking spray.
3. In a small saucepan, heat the Coca-Cola®, cocoa powder, and butter over medium heat until the butter is melted.
4. Add the sugars and whisk until dissolved.
5. Remove from the heat and let cool. In a large bowl, whisk the flour, baking soda, and salt together.
6. In a small bowl, whisk the eggs until just beaten, then whisk them into the cooled cocoa mixture until combined.
7. Gently fold the flour mixture into the cocoa mixture.

8. The batter will be slightly lumpy—do not overbeat, as it could cause the cake to be tough. Pour the batter into the prepared cupcake liners/tin and bake for about 20 minutes, rotating the pan halfway through the baking time, until a small skewer inserted into the cake comes out clean.
9. Transfer the cupcakes to a wire rack to cool completely.
10. In a medium bowl, beat whipping cream, powdered sugar and vanilla extract until medium peaks form.
11. Transfer to pastry bag with a star tip.
12. In a circular motion, pipe on whipped cream and top each one with one cherry.

Coca-Cola® Cupcakes with Salted Peanut Butter Frosting

Ingredients

Cupcakes:

1 cup Coca-Cola® at room temperature

1/2 cup unsweetened cocoa powder

4 tbsp. unsalted butter, cut into pieces

1/2 cup plus 2 tbsp. granulated sugar

1/4 cup firmly packed dark brown sugar

1 cup all-purpose flour

1/2 tsp. plus 1/8 tsp. baking soda

1/2 tsp. salt

1 eggs

Salted peanut butter frosting:

4 cups powdered sugar

1 cup unsalted butter, softened

1 cup creamy peanut butter

1/4 tsp salt

3-4 tbsp. heavy cream

Sea salt for sprinkling

Chocolate sprinkles

Ground salted peanuts

Directions

1.   Preheat the oven to 350F. Line a cupcake pan with baking papers.

2.   In a small saucepan, heat Coca-Cola®, cocoa powder, and butter over medium heat until butter is melted. Add sugars and whisk until dissolved. Remove from heat and let cool.

3. In a large bowl, whisk flour, baking soda, and salt together.

4. In a small bowl, whisk egg until just beaten, then whisk them into the cooled cocoa mixture until combined. Gently stir flour mixture into cocoa mixture.

5. Use a 1/4 cup measure to pour batter into the cupcake papers. Bake cupcakes for 25 minutes or until cake springs back when pressed in the middle.

6. Allow cupcakes to cool completely before frosting.

Note: Diet Coca Cola® can NOT be used as a substitute for regular Coca Cola® in this recipe.

Salted peanut butter frosting:
1. In the bowl of a stand mixer fitted with a whisk attachment, combine powdered sugar, butter, peanut butter and salt.
2. Mix on low speed until just combined, then switch to high speed.
3. Add heavy cream one tablespoon and beat until mixture is lightened and smooth.
4. Transfer to a piping bag or zip-top bag with the corner snipped.
5. Pipe onto cooled cupcakes.
6. Garnish with sprinkles, ground peanuts and a sprinkling of sea salt.

UK Version Coca-Cola® Cake

Ingredients

For the cake

200 g (7 oz.) plain flour

250 g (1/2 lb.) golden caster sugar

1/2 teaspoon bicarbonate of soda

1/4 teaspoon salt

1 large egg

125 ml (1/2 cup) buttermilk

1 teaspoon vanilla extract

125 g (4 oz.) unsalted butter

2 tablespoons cocoa powder

175 ml (3/4 cup) Coca-Cola®

(22-23 cm spring form pan, lined with foil to prevent the batter leaking, then greased)

For the icing

225 g (7 oz.) icing sugar

2 tablespoons (30g) butter

3 tablespoons (45ml) Coca-Cola®

1 tablespoon (15 mL) cocoa powder

1/2 teaspoon vanilla extract

Directions

1. Preheat the oven to 180/gas mark 4/ 350 F and put in a baking sheet at the same time.
2. In a large bowl, combine the flour, sugar, bicarb and salt.

3. In a measuring jug, beat the egg, buttermilk and vanilla.

4. In a heavy-based saucepan, melt the butter, cocoa and Coca-Cola®, heating it gently.

5. Pour into the dry ingredients, stir well with a wooden spoon, and then add the liquid ingredients from the jug, beating until it is well blended.

6. Pour into the prepared tin and bake on the warm sheet for 40 minutes or until a tester comes out clean.

7. Leave to stand for 15 minutes in the tin before unmoulding.

8. Then unclip, unwrap and turn out on a wire rack, making sure you've got a sheet of newspaper or something underneath the rack to catch any icing that drips through.

9. Sieve the icing sugar and set aside for the moment. In a heavy-based saucepan, combine the butter, Coca-Cola® and cocoa and stir over a low heat until the butter has melted.

10. Remove from the heat, add the vanilla, and spoon in the sieved icing sugar, beating as you do so, until you've got a good, spreadable, but still a bit runny, icing.

11. Pour this icing over the cake, while the cake is still warm, spread gently and leave till cool before transferring to the plate on which you're serving it.

Coca-Cola® Poke Cake

Ingredients

For the cake:

2 cups all-purpose flour

1 teaspoon baking soda

3/4 teaspoon salt

1/4 cup unsweetened cocoa powder

1/2 cup butter, at room temperature

1/2 cup vegetable oil

2 cups sugar

1 teaspoon vanilla extract

2 eggs

1 cup Coca-Cola® at room temperature

For the glaze:

4 cups powdered sugar

1/4 cup unsweetened cocoa powder

1/2 cup butter softened

1/2 cup Coca-Cola® at room temperature

Direction

1. Preheat oven to 350 degrees. Grease and flour a 13x9 baking pan; set aside.

2. Sift together flour, baking soda, salt and cocoa powder; set aside.

3. Using an electric mixer at medium speed, beat together butter, oil, sugar, vanilla and eggs until creamy (about 2 minutes).

4.   Add Coca-Cola® and mix on low speed. With mixer still set at low, add flour mixture and continue mixing for one minute or until all ingredients thoroughly combined.

5.   Pour batter into prepared pan.

6.   Bake at 350 degrees for 30-40 minutes or until toothpick inserted in the middle comes out clean.

7.   Once done, poke holes in the cake at about 1-inch intervals using a serving fork, skewer or whatever gets it done (try not to use a regular fork if the tines are pretty close together because it might tear up the cake too much); set aside and make the glaze.

To make the glaze:

1.   Sift together powdered sugar and cocoa powder; set aside.

2.   In a medium-sized saucepan heat butter and Coca-Cola® over medium-high heat until boiling.

3.   Once mixture starts to boil, continue cooking for one minute.

4.   Remove pan from heat and whisk in sugar and cocoa mixture until smooth.

5.   Slowly pour glaze over cake. If your cake isn't completely level, using potholders to handle the pan, slowly tilt cake back and forth, forward and back until all the glaze has soaked into the cake. This prevents all the glaze from settling into the low spots.

6.   Cool at room temperature for 1-2 hours before serving.

Coca-Cola® Cake Version 3

Prep Time: 15 minutes

Cook Time: 35 minutes

Total Time: 1 hour

Ingredients

2 cups all-purpose flour

1 teaspoon baking soda

1 1/2 cups sugar

1 cup butter

1 1/2 cup mini marshmallows

1/4 cup cocoa

1 cup Coca-Cola® at room temperature

1/2 cup buttermilk

2 eggs

2 teaspoons vanilla

Icing

1/2 cup butter softened

1/3 cup Coca-Cola® at room temperature

3 tablespoons cocoa

4 cups powdered sugar

1 tablespoon vanilla

1 cup pecans, coarsely chopped

Instructions

1. In a large bowl, combine the flour and baking soda. Blend well. Stir in sugar.

2. In a medium saucepan, combine 1 cup butter and marshmallows.

3. Cook over medium heat until the marshmallows are melted. Remove from heat and stir in cocoa. Set aside.

4. Add Coca-Cola®, buttermilk, eggs, and vanilla to the dry ingredients and stir until just combined.

5. Slowly add butter/marshmallow/cocoa mixture. Stir until combined

6. Pour into a greased 9X13 pan and bake at 350 degrees F for 30 to 35 minutes.

7. For icing, combine butter, Coca-Cola®, and cocoa in a medium saucepan, heat until just boiling. Remove from heat and slowly stir in vanilla and sugar.

8. Pour over warm cake. Sprinkle with chopped pecans.

Coca Cola® Carrot Cake

Cooking Time: 50 min

Ingredients

2 cups flour, sifted

1 teaspoon baking soda

1/2 teaspoon salt

2 tablespoons cocoa

3 eggs

1 1/2 cup sugar

1/2 cup vegetable oil

3/4 cup Coca-Cola®

1 1/2 teaspoon vanilla extract

2 1/4 cups raw carrots, grated

1 cup nuts, chopped

1 cup coconut, flaked

3/4 cup sugar

2 teaspoons cocoa

6 tablespoons Coca-Cola®

6 tablespoons butter

1 tablespoon light corn syrup

1/2 teaspoon vanilla

Instructions

1. Mix all the dry ingredients together.

2. Beat the eggs well; add sugar, oil, 3/4 cup Cola®, and vanilla and beat well.

3. Stir in the dry ingredients until smooth, then add the carrots, nuts and coconut. Mix well.

4. Bake in a greased and lightly floured 13 x 9 pan in a preheated 350~F oven for 40-50 minutes, until cake tests done.

5. Remove from oven and prick hot cake all over with a fork, then pour the Cola® syrup slowly, evenly over the top.

6. Serve warm or room temperature with lightly sweetened-vanilla flavored whipped cream.

Coca Cola® Syrup

1. Combine sugar, cocoa, Coca Cola®, butter and corn syrup in saucepan; bring to a boil over medium heat, stirring constantly.

2. Boil, stirring, until thick and syrupy, about 5 minutes.

3. Add vanilla extract. Remove from heat and pour, hot, over hot cake.

Coca-Cola® Cake Recipe

TOTAL TIME: 1 hour and 15 minutes

Prep Time: 30 min

Cook Time: 45 min

Ingredients

2 cups sugar

2 cups all-purpose flour

1 cup Coca-Cola®

1 ½ cups small marshmallows

½ cups butter or margarine

½ cups vegetable oil

3 tablespoons cocoa

1 teaspoon baking soda

½ cups buttermilk

2 eggs

1 teaspoon vanilla extract

½ cups butter

3 tablespoons cocoa

6 tablespoons Coca-Cola®

1 box (16-ounces) confectioners' sugar

1 teaspoon vanilla extract

1 cup chopped pecans

Preparation

1. Preheat oven to 350 degrees.

2. In a bowl, sift the sugar and flour.

3. Add marshmallows.

4. In a saucepan, mix the butter, oil, cocoa and Coca-Cola®. Bring to a boil and pour over dry ingredients; blend well.

5. Dissolve baking soda in buttermilk just before adding to batter along with eggs and vanilla extract, mixing well.

6. Pour into a well-greased 9- by-13-inch pan and bake 35 to 45 minutes. Remove from oven and frost immediately.

Coca-Cola® Cake Frosting

To make frosting, combine the 1/2 cup butter, 3 tablespoons cocoa and 6 tablespoons of Coca-Cola® in a saucepan. Bring to a boil and pour over confectioners' sugar, blending well. Add vanilla extract and pecans. Spread over hot cake. When cool, cut into squares and serve.

Bing Cherry Jello Mold with Coca Cola®

Ingredients

1 (12 fluid ounce) can Coca Cola® at room temperature

1 (16.5 ounce) can pitted Bing cherries

1 (20 ounce) can crushed pineapple with juice

1 (6 ounce) package black cherry flavored gelatin mix

1 cup chopped pecans

Instructions

1. Drain pineapple. Drain the cherries and save their juice.

2. In a saucepan combine the reserved cherry juice with the coke.

3. Heat until boiling then stir in the gelatin.

4. Mix until gelatin is dissolved.

5. Remove from the heat and stir in the drained pineapple, drained cherries and chopped pecans.

6. Pour mixture into a mold sprayed with a nonstick cooking spray and refrigerate for at least 24 hours before serving.

Cherry Coke Salad

Preparation Time: 2 hr.

Ingredients

1 can 40 ounces dark pitted cherries

1 3 ounce package cherry gelatin

1 can 20 ounces crushed pineapple

1 cup Coca Cola® at room temperature

1/2 cup pecans, chopped

Instructions

1. Heat cherries and their juice to boiling.
2. Remove from heat and add gelatin. Stir.
3. Add pineapple including juice. Pour in coke and nuts. Pour into an oiled 6-cup mold.
4. Let cool, then refrigerate at least 2 hours or until set. Serve cold.

Coca Cola® and Cherry Jello Salad

Ingredients

1 cup Coca Cola® soda

1 3 ounce package cherry jello

3 ounces cream cheese

1 small can crushed pineapple, reserve juice

1 small can black cherries, reserve juice

1/2 cup combined reserved pineapple and cherry syrup from the two cans above

Instructions

1. Heat Coca Cola® on stovetop and dissolve gelatin in it.
2. Remove from heat.
3. Stir in softened cream cheese
4. Stir fruit and reserved fruit juices
5. Place mixture in gelatin mold or glass bowl and chill very well until set.
6. Serve topped with whipped cream.

Coca Cola® Brownies

Prep time: 10 minutes

Total time: 40 minutes

Ingredients

1 1/4 cups (6 1/4 ounces) all-purpose flour

1 2/3 cups (12 1/4 ounces) sugar

2/3 cup cocoa powder

1/2 teaspoon salt

1/2 teaspoon baking powder

1 can (12 ounces) Coca Cola® at room temperature

Directions

1. Adjust oven rack to middle position and preheat oven to 350°F. Either grease baking pan with oil or cover with tin foil.

2. In a large bowl, stir together flour, sugar, cocoa, salt, and baking powder until combined.

3. Add Coca Cola®, a little at a time because it will foam, until incorporated and batter forms.

4. Pour batter into pan and bake until a tester inserted into the middle of the pan comes out clean, about 30 minutes. Top will be slightly sticky.

5. Let cool completely in pan then cut into squares.

Out of this World Coca Cola® Brownies

Cooking time: 30 minutes

Ingredients

2 Cups Flour

2 Cups White Sugar

1 Cup. Butter

4 Tablespoons Cocoa

1Cup Coca Cola at room temperature

1/2 Cup Buttermilk

2 Eggs

1 Teaspoon Baking Soda

2 Cups Mini Marshmallows

1 Teaspoon Pure Vanilla

DIRECTIONS

1. Heat Oven to 350 degrees

2. Sift together the sugar and flour

3. Heat together butter, cocoa and Coca Cola to boiling; pour over sugar and flour.

4. Mix together buttermilk, eggs, baking soda, vanilla & marshmallows and slowly add to mixture mixing well.

5. Batter will be thin.

6. Pour into a greased baking pan with an edge and bake for 30 minutes.

7. Carefully remove from oven, allow to cool and then serve.

Coca-Cola® Jello Salad with Cherries

Ingredients

6 ounces cherry-flavored Jello (not sugar-free)

1 cup boiling water

1 cup regular Coca-Cola® at room temperature

1 14.5 ounce can red tart pitted cherries in water

1 8-ounce can crushed pineapple

Instructions

1. Boil 1 cup water on stovetop
2. In a large heat safe bowl, add the package of Jello.
3. Once the water is rolling, pour one cup of the boiling water over the jello and stir until dissolved.
4. Stir in the Coca-Cola®. Pour in slowly as it may foam up fast.
5. Cover and refrigerate mixture until partially firm, about 45 minutes.
6. Stir the Jello every 10 minutes or so; you want it a thickened but not set.
7. Meanwhile, add the can of cherries to a food processor or blender.
8. Pulse in one-second intervals, about 3-5 pulses, until the cherries are chopped into small pieces but not blended.
9. Once the Jello mixture has thickened, stir in the chopped cherries and its juice, pineapple and its juice.
10. Pour into a jello mold, bowl, Bundt pan, or 2-quart casserole dish.
11. Cover tightly and refrigerate until set, at least 4 hours, overnight, or up to 2 days before serving.
12. Remove salad from the mold by inverting onto a serving platter.
13. Serve cold.

Note- you can pour the Jello into individual size containers too.

Bing Cherry Jello Mold with Coca Cola®

Ingredients

1 (12 fluid ounce) can Coca Cola®

1 (16.5 ounce) can pitted Bing cherries

1 (20 ounce) can crushed pineapple with juice

1 (6 ounce) package black cherry flavored gelatin mix

1 cup chopped pecans

Instructions

1. Drain pineapple. Drain the cherries and save their juice.

2. In a saucepan combine the reserved cherry juice with the Coke.

3. Heat until boiling then stir in the gelatin.

4. Mix until gelatin is dissolved.

5. Remove from the heat and stir in the drained pineapple, drained cherries and chopped pecans.

6. Pour mixture into a mold sprayed with a nonstick cooking spray and refrigerate for at least 24 hours before serving.

Diet Coke 'Almost Brownies' Recipe

TOTAL TIME: 1 hour

Prep Time: 15 min

Cook Time: 45 min

Ingredients

1 box of chocolate cake mix

1 can Diet Coke at room temperature

1 small package of Instant sugar-free pudding mix

1 container of fat-free chilled whipped topping

Preparation

1. Mix cake mix and Diet Coke together.

2. Bake in an oil-sprayed 9 x 13 pan.

3. Cook at 350 degrees for approximately 45 minutes until slightly underdone.

4. Cool.

5. Frosting: Put 1 small package of sugar-free, fat-free instant chocolate pudding mix into one 8-ounce container of fat-free chilled whipped topping. Mix well. Frost the cake and cut into squares. They taste like brownies, but without all the fat.

Cherry Coke Salad

Preparation Time: 2 hr.

Ingredients

40 ounces can dark pitted cherries

3 ounces package cherry gelatin

20 ounces crushed pineapple

1 cup Coca Cola®

1/2 cup pecans, chopped

Instructions

1. Heat cherries and their juice to boiling.
2. Remove from heat and add gelatin. Stir.
3. Add pineapple, juice and all. Pour in coke and nuts. Pour into an oiled 6-cup mold.
4. Let cool, then refrigerate at least 2 hours or until set. Serve cold.

Thank You

Thank you for purchasing this book. I hope you enjoyed the recipe selection as much as I have enjoyed compiling it over the years.

If you have a Coca Cola recipe that you would like to share with me, you can reach me via

LoeraPublishing@hotmail.com

I am also on Pinterest www.Pinterest.com/Loera and have more Coca Cola recipes listed there on one of my boards.

Sincerely,

Diana

www.ingramcontent.com/pod-product-compliance
Lightning Source LLC
Chambersburg PA
CBHW041549220426
43666CB00002B/20